Behind the Basket

Behind the Basket
An Ethnography of the Women's National Basketball
Association
Joseph C Wilson

Chapter 1: Warm-Up

The 19th Century in Western Europe and North America was a century of shifting from agrarian cultural practices to industrial economies. That industry depended on a system of production capable of producing replaceable parts- such as screws and nails made exactly like every other screw or nail. Mass production of replaceable parts gave way to a philosophy of Modernism- and not just in the production of tangible goods. Art and entertainment movements entered the modern world during the time- including sport.

In 1896; France, Great Britain, and the United States banded together to re-spark the Olympic flame ignited millennia before to bring ancient athletics into the modern world. The idea was simple: assemble the greatest known athletes in the world to compete in athletic competitions with clear and uniform rules and regulations to see who would win. A modernized system of rewards and punishments accompanied the competition including standardized medals (gold, silver, and bronze for first, second, and third place finishes) for rewards; and penalties, fines, and potential bans for punishments.

The first Modern Olympics included athletes from fourteen countries and took place in the ancient homeland of the games- Greece. In the forty-three events of the competition, there were a total of two hundred forty-one athletes.[1] The new competition revolutionized the sports industry. Before the Modern Olympics emerged, sports existed more to pass the time rather than establish a series for the entertainment industry. It seemed however, that sport could not escape the growth of Modernism expanding into the daily facets of the industrialized world.

Half a decade into the 20th Century however is when Modernization became a dominant paradigm in the growing industrial world. Following the events of the Second World War and the expansion of Communism, modernization of more than replaceable parts began affecting sport. Humans throughout Europe,

---

[1] Olympic.org. 2019

Asia, and North America quickly found themselves becoming replaceable parts in their modern world. Ideas of race, political affiliation, and standards of living began shaping a world where individuals found themselves locking into socially stratified classes for the proposed betterment of their respective societies- and the Cold War fueled that government endorsed conformist philosophy.[2]

Cold War Era sports had heavily modernized sociology. A perfect example of this is with soccer. Athletes in soccer play by a set of rules and regulations codified and uniform throughout both the club level and the international level. There are clear rules about what qualifications an athlete needs to compete for club-level league and at the international level- and this is no surprise. While soccer may have originated from an ancestral sport in Medieval England, the sport realistically developed under the modernization of the international organization FIFA.

This modernization of sport works well for athletes too. Having a clear set of rules that applies to every game and every level of the sport allows an athlete to be fully aware of what rules and regulations they must play under while competing in multiple games. If not for that modernization, the athlete would practically be playing a different sport every single game. The issue however is when more rules become modernized. During the immediate aftermath of the end of the Cold War (the 1990's), athletes began discovering the effects modernization had on their characters.

Part of the problem with the modernization of human resources is that humans are- to greatly oversimplify- massively diverse. From the individual level to the societal level, humans and their cultures have a tremendous diversity in how they interpret and experience the world around them. As a result, modernizing world-view and experience can dissolve that diversity and homogenize individuals without their consent. In sports specifically, athletes are typecast as children by their subculture executive (typically a coach or instructor) decides what that athlete will be as an adult through a process known as "biobanding."

Modernization of youth sports might separate boys from girls, and typically further separates those groups by age. The idea is simple- kids that have not gone through puberty yet probably should

---

[2] Engerman, Gilman, Haefele, & Latham. 2003.

not be competing against kids who already have. The problem is that modern definitions of puberty set a rigid age (or in some cases grade level) for when puberty happens. What this means is that a twelve year old girl is not going to compete against a ten year-old girl in a soccer game- to make the game a more fair competition. The problem is that some girls enter puberty earlier, and others enter puberty later than the modernized age definition.

Biobanding is the process by which athletes and instructors further categorize their young athletes by biological-based skill. A twelve year-old boy that plays hockey that has already hit puberty might be a full foot taller and tremendously stronger than his pre-pubescent peer of the same age. Putting that stronger player on the field could lead to physical injuries for pre-pubescent peers, and even long-term feelings in the kid feeling as though he will never be good enough. That could even cause him to quit sports entirely.

Modernization of definitions of age is especially hard on women and girls. The process greatly favors girls who mature later than average in sports like gymnastics or figure skating- which favor slender forms. Sports that favor strength and power- such as tennis- often favor girls who mature earlier than average. Biobanding attempts to change this by categorizing athletes based on individual definitions, rather than modern ones. Athletes are more equally pitted against each other in brackets based not on legal age, but biological development.[3]

This system of categorization and regulation of sport falls more in line with Postmodernism. At its most basic definition, Postmodernism is a philosophy of non-identifiability. The concept is used to describe things that cannot be defined by a modern sense and instead consists of a series of changing and diverse definitions. Imagine two people are standing in front of a painting arguing over what color the painting is. That painting might appear as two different images to the two people looking at it. Humans themselves are often hard to categorize, and that difficulty in modernizing humans has spread to sports through the growing post-modernization of sports.

That is where the WNBA came in. During the 1990's when the WNBA launched as a women's basketball league in the United

---

[3] Cumming, Malina, & Rogol. 2018.

States, the organization attempted to create a mirror of the men's league for women athletes. A similar series of rules and regulations mirrored the men's game, and the league even targeted the same audience in the hopes of bringing NBA fans into WNBA stadiums. That Modernist approach didn't work however, and nearly destroyed the young league before the WNBA decided on a different strategy.

Because the early league depended on stipend support from the NBA to survive, the WNBA had to mirror the men's league to a degree. This presented unique challenges to the women's league however. Many of the NBA investors were conservative men and many of the NBA teams existed in traditionally conservative cities (think San Antonio and Salt Lake City). Many of those conservative investors were not content with adult women playing professional sports and became even more dissenting when women in the WNBA began coming out as gay.[4]

In response, the WNBA began distancing themselves from the NBA and instead focused on targeting the fans unique to women's basketball. Teams shifted away from cities with men's teams to cities with historic LGBT and feminist history instead and opened an avenue for postmodernism in women's sports as the first major women's sports league in the United States. Most of the founding players of the WNBA have left the sport behind them now, though a few that played during the demographic shift of the early 2000's are still competing as the eldest generation of WNBA players.

As those athletes slowly leave the game as the last players left from the shift from modern women's basketball to postmodern women's basketball, the league increasingly deals with the balance of modernism and postmodernism. Modern definitions of rules and regulations often check the increasingly unique demands of individuals and teams. The 2019 WNBA season saw the proverbial tug-of-war between these two competing philosophies both on and off the court- making the WNBA perhaps the best example of the conflict and balance of Modernism and Postmodernism in sport.

"Never Be the Same" Camila Cabello

---

[4] Evans. 19-126. 2006.

During the summer of 2018, I packed my bags one final time as I left Alaska behind me. I was starting a new chapter in my life and would move to Hawaii. After a brief stay in Seattle for a final research trip on the Seattle Reign soccer team and a brief stop in Southern California to visit family, I stopped by the hostel I stayed at during my surfing research trip to San Clemente. The hostel was much more quiet than the last time I visited. There were few other guests, and there was no more championship tour event at Lower Trestles.

I was wrong to assume before returning that I would find the same scene at the hostel as I had enjoyed during my first stay. A different set of guests and staff was there; and none of them were comparable to the Brazilian judo fighter, the Canadian zip-liner, or the Floridian surf photographer I had met before. It was a perfect example of the postmodernism of reality. The same location seemed to be different each time I visited.

After San Clemente, I returned to Los Angeles and boarded a plane for Maui where I would once again visit an old hostel from my surfing research field studies. I started working for the hostel in Wailuku I stayed at as a guest the year before and found the scene different from my first stay as House of Trestles was. While spending my days vacuuming floors and mopping bathrooms, I spent my evenings watching Seattle Storm basketball games- including an incredible championship game.

In 2018, the Seattle Storm earned the WNBA championship title off the talent of team members and coaching staff that delivered the team from a poor 2017 performance to a 2018 championship title. By all means, the team would be on track to follow their successful season with another. In practice, modernism is that idea that if a piece of a machine has to be replaced, the machine will perform equally with the replacement part. Postmodernism means the machine never performs the same way- even with all the same parts. The 2019 Seattle Storm season would test the modernism and postmodernism of the league.

During preseason developments, two of the teams top awarded players- Sue Bird and Breanna Stewart- announced they would miss either all or a majority of the 2019 season due to injuries. Breanna Steward ruptured her Achilles Tendon while playing in a European basketball league during the championship game. Stewart had earned the 2018 MVP and Finals MVP awards for her WNBA performance as well as Olympic gold for Team USA.[5]

I understood what it was like to suffer a season-ending injury. While not physical, my time in Hawaii was unpredictably debilitating. My time on what I thought would be paradise was surprisingly depressing. Maui's crime rate was on the rise, livable wages were impossible to find, and my job at the hostel came with strange guests and unprofessional management. While I was able to find escape on beaches with admittedly beautiful women (so not all bad!), I could not escape the curse of a voodoo witch doctor (true story) or the wrath of an unusually cold winter.

When I arrived in Seattle at the end of March, I had spent nearly all of the little money I had and was broken. The voodoo witchdoctor's curse was still active, and I was in dire need of a morale boost. I managed to get another hostel job at a hostel in Fremont and began setting to work on researching the Seattle Storm. I wouldn't be able to do the study as planned because of my lack of funding, but I had to find a way to salvage my research.

With both Sue Bird and Breanna Stewart out for the foreseeable season, commentators placed their eyes on Crystal Langhorne as the core player for the team going into the 2019 season.[6] The Storm re-signed Langhorne and Mercedes Russell. The 2019 season would be Langhorne's sixth season with the Storm and the twelfth season in the league- making her a critical veteran for the under-strength team.[7] During the 2019 WNBA draft, the Storm acquired center Ezi Magbegor from Australia, forward Anriel Howard from Mississippi State, and guard Macy Miller from South Dakota State. The bulk of the team's weight however would fall on the middle players- those athletes not yet experienced enough to earn the veteran title, but by no means rookies.

During a preseason game against the Phoenix Mercury on 15 May, the Storm performed admirably without Steward and Bird in a loss to Phoenix. During the first quarter, Phoneix led marginally twenty-five to twenty-four. At the end of the half, the Mercury led fifty-one to forty-eight. In the third quarter, the Mercury led sixty-

---

[5] WNBA. 2019.
[6] Smith. 2019.
[7] WNBA. 2019.

seven to sixty-four. The game ended with a three-point difference for a Storm loss eighty-four to eighty-seven. The Storm had other missing factors for the game. Sami Whitcomb and Alysha Clarke both missed the game, and coach Dan Hughes was absent while receiving treatment for cancer.

Two days later, the Storm lost to the Los Angeles Sparks in a game on 17 May. The Sparks led the first quarter nineteen to eighteen, then finished the half behind Seattle forty-four to forty-nine. Los Angeles pulled ahead in the third quarter to bring the game to seventy-three to fifty-nine before winning the game ninety-two to eighty-five. Projections for the Storm's 2019 season were rough to read. Positive comments about the 2018 season were mostly linked to players that would be missing the season. The *modern* team however would put to the test its ability to substitute its big name players with less famous athletes and achieve a similar result.

While Sue Bird and Breanna Stewart would be missing the 2019 season, the team planned on relying on Jewell Loyd, Jordin Canada, Natasha Howard, Mercedes Russell, and Crystal Langhorne as their returning players and Anriel Howard as their new team member. The team hoped coach Dan Hughes would be back during the season from cancer treatment to organize the team, but would have to rely on assistant coaches to lead the team in his absence.[8]

"Most Girls" Hailee Steinfeld

On paper; the Storm's 2019 roster included guards Sue Bird, Jordin Canada, Blake Dietrick, Jewell Loyd, Mercedes Russell, Shavonte Zellous, and Sami Whitcomb (who also served as a forward); forwards Alysha Clark, Natasha Howard, Kaleena Masqueda-Lewis, Breanna Steward, and Crystal Langhorne (who also served as a center); and center Courtney Paris. In practice, the Storm would end up relying on Canada, Loyd, Langhorne, and Howard to lead the team in the season.

Sue Bird began her career in the WNBA in 2002 with the Seattle Storm whom she has played for during her entire league career. Bird came to the WNBA from the University of Connecticut- a dynasty in women's college basketball. During her time with the WNBA, she also played several seasons abroad with Ekaterinburg,

---

[8] Martin. 2019.

Sparta & K, and Dynamo in Russia. Before the 2019 season, Bird was a three-time WNBA champion (2004, 2010, and 2018), was the all-time league assist leader, and was a number one draft pick.[9]

Jordin Canada started her WNBA career in 2018 with the Storm and played in every game of the season save for one. She played one season abroad for Wisla Can-Pack Krakow in Poland and played for UCLA before hitting the professionals. Canada also has a special place in my heart as a fellow anthropology student athlete (also including fencer Mariel Zagunis!).[10]

Blake Dietrick played briefly in the WNBA in 2016 including a training camp with the Seattle Storm and a few games with the San Antonio Stars (Las Vegas Aces as of 2019). Dietrick played overseas before her WNBA career with Cestica Orvieto in Italy, then again in her break from the WNBA for Bendigo Spirit in Australia and AO Dafni Agioy Dimitriou in Greece. Dietrick returned to the WNBA in 2018 to play for the Atlanta Wings before joining the Storm for the 2019 season.[11]

Jewell Loyd started her professional career in 2015 with the Seattle Storm and has been on the team since. She was drafted first overall during the 2015 draft from Notre Dame. Loyd has played on a few overseas teams including Galatasaray and Botas in Turkey, Shanxi in China, and Winnus in South Korea. Loyd has also played for the US national team including the 2018 world championship team.[12]

Mercedes Russell joined the WNBA in 2018 with the Seattle Storm and played for Wisla Can Pack in Poland overseas. Russell played for the University of Tennessee before becoming a professional athlete, but did not receive much publicity before the 2019 season.[13] Due to Sue Bird and Breanna Stewart missing 2019, Russell would end up playing an integral part of the 2019 Seattle Storm team.

While born in Florida, Shavonte Zellous was the sole Croatian national (obtained for the ability to play for the Croatian

---

9 WNBA. 2019.

10 WNBA. 2019.

11 WNBA. 2019.

12 WNBA. 2019.

13 WNBA. 2019.

national team) on the 2019 Storm team. Zellous joined the WNBA in 2009 after playing for Pittsburg in college. The athlete joined the Storm for the 2019 season from the New York Liberty and has played for several international teams including Besiktas Istanbul, Adana Ankara, Fenerbahce Istanbul, Galatasaray Istanbul, and Mersin Mersin in Turkey; TTT-Tiga Riga in Latvia; and AS Ramat Hasharon Electra in Israel.[14]

Sami Whitcomb came to the WNBA from the University of Washington and joined in 2010 with the Chicago Sky- though the team waived her before the start of the regular season. Whitcomb left the league for nearly a decade by playing overseas with ChemCats Chemnitz and Wolfenbuttel Wildcats in Germany, and Rockingham Flames and Perth Lynx in Australia. Witcomb rejoined the WNBA in 2017 by joining the Seattle Storm and earned a championship title in 2018. Following her return to the WNBA, Whitcomb also played overseas including her Australian team and with Montpellier in France.[15]

Alysha Clark started her WNBA career with the Storm in 2012 after playing overseas for Hapoel Rishon LeZion and Ramat Hasharon in Israel. Clark played for Seattle in every season of her WNBA career, but continued to play in overseas leagues with Ramat Hasharon and Maccabi Ashdod in Israel, Adana in Turkey, CCC Polkawice in Poland, and Lyon ASVEL Feminin in France. Clark played college ball for Middle Tennessee State and earned a WNBA championship title with the Storm in 2018.[16]

Natasha Howard started her WNBA career in 2014 with the Indiana Fever, earned a championship title in 2017 with the Minnesota Lynx, then joined the Storm for the 2018 championship season. Howard played overseas with Elitzur Ramla in Israel, KB Stars in South Korea, Famila Schio in Italy, Samsung Blue Minx in South Korea, and Zhejiang in China. The athlete entered her professional career after playing for Florida State University.[17]

Kaleena Masqueda-Lewis joined the WNBA with the Seattle Storm in 2015 after playing for Connecticut in college. She was

---

[14] WNBA. 2019.

[15] WNBA. 2019.

[16] WNBA. 2019.

[17] WNBA. 2019.

drafted third overall to Seattle in the 2015 draft and has played for Charleville-Mezieres and Flammes in France overseas. Masqueda-Lewis was another athlete who did not receive much attention or playing time before the 2019 season, but did see a career best during the 2018 championship season with Seattle.[18]

Breanna Stewart joined the WNBA in 2016 with the Seattle Storm as the first overall draft pick for the year. Stewart played for Connecticut in college before earning the Rookie of the Year award for her 2016 WNBA performance. Stewart was an integral part of the Storm's 2018 championship season and earned both the MVP award for the season and the MVP award for the finals. The young athlete played for Shanghai in China overseas and Kursk Russia in the EuroLeague- with whom she obtained her 2019 season ending injury.[19]

Crystal Langhorne joined the WNBA in 2008 with the Washington Mystics before earning the Most Improved Player award in 2009. Langhorne moved to Seattle in 2014 from Washington and also played an integral part in the 2018 championship season for the Storm. Langhorne has played several seasons overseas including with Teo Vilnius in Lithuania, Rivas Ecopolis in Spain, UMMS Ekaterinburg and Dynamo Moscow in Russia, Istanbul University in Turkey, Good Angels in Slovakia, Heilongjiang in China, and Sopron Basket in Hungary.[20]

Courtney Paris joined the WNBA in 2009 with the Sacramento Monarchs before the team eventually dissolved. Paris joined the Seattle Storm in 2018 after moving from the Dallas Wings and earned a championship title with the Storm in 2018. Paris has also played in several overseas leagues including with Maccabi Ashdod in Israel; Rivas Ecopolis in Spain; and Botas, Mersin, Istanbul Universitesi SK, and Hatay BSB in Turkey.[21]

"Dancing in the Dark" Rihanna

The Seattle Storm played three regular season games in May. Without Breanna Stewart, Sue Bird, or coach Dan Hughes; players

---

[18] WNBA. 2019.

[19] WNBA. 2019.

[20] WNBA. 2019.

[21] WNBA. 2019.

and assistant coaches alike scrambled to develop a new strategy with their adjusted starting line-up players. On 25 May, the Storm played the Phoenix Mercury in Seattle. Actually, the Storm played in Everett north of Seattle. Key Arena- where the team played home games for years- was under renovation for the entirety of the season. Instead, the Storm would play at a combination of two arenas- one in Everett and one at the University of Washington in Seattle.

The Storm was not the only Seattle sports team to move for the 2019 season. The city's NWSL team- the Reign- moved to Tacoma. The hope was that moving to a larger stadium would attract more ticket buyers and would attract more of a family demographic by moving the team to a suburban setting. The Storm's partial move to Everett could attract more families in the suburban setting, and the move to the university campus could attract more college students to attend games.

On 25 May, the Storm were down during the first quarter sixteen to twenty-three and finished the half tied at thirty-two points. During the third quarter, the Mercury fell behind to a forty-eight to fifty-six lag before losing to the Storm sixty-eight to seventy-seven. Natasha Howard carried the Storm through the game as the points leader- scoring twenty-one points during the game. In contrast, the Mercury points leader was DeWanna Bonner with thirty-one.

That might have been why Seattle won though. The Storm consistently played a strategy of subbing out their athletes, then subbing them back in to prevent exhaustion. This is a common strategy in warfare- something sport was invented to reenact peacefully across cultures and history. In Ancient Rome, imperial legions would employ battle formations where the soldier at the front of the line would move to the back- preventing any one soldier from fighting during one hundred percent of the battle.[22] The Seattle Storm employed the tactic during every game (and most other teams do too)- which also prevents any points leader in a game from making any massive impact on the score.

If one player scores nearly half of their entire team's points, then that player is either playing too much (and could risk obtaining an injury) or the other players are not playing to their fullest potential. While Howard scored roughly one fourth of her team's

---

[22] Know the Romans. 2019.

points, Bonner scored nearly half of hers. Jewell Loyd for example, scored seventeen points in the game- showing a shallow disparity in the first and second place scorers for Seattle.

After the first week of the regular season, the power rankings showed the twelve teams of the league following their opening games. Seattle sat in seventh place behind Las Vegas, Connecticut, Washington, Los Angeles, Phoenix, and Atlanta and ahead of Minnesota, Indiana, Dallas, Chicago, and New York.[23] (Seattle's placement behind Phoenix was likely due to their preseason loss).

On 29 May, the Seattle Storm met The Minnesota Lynx in Minneapolis for their second regular season game. After the first quarter, the Lynx led the Storm a whopping twenty-two to nine. The Storm finally built some momentum during the second quarter, but remained behind going into the half twenty-six to thirty-nine. In the fourth quarter, the Lynx continued to lead with sixty-one to forty-six; then finished the game with a seventy-two to sixty-one win against Seattle. Natasha Howard was the Seattle points leader again with eighteen points (roughly 3/10) and Odyssey Sims led the Lynx with only fifteen points (roughly 1/5).

The game highlighted both teams' strategy of relying on the modernism of teamwork rather than the postmodernism of individualism on the court, and Minnesota was better at it than Seattle. While the Storm continued to rely on individual athletes to balance teamwork on their team, they just did not have the star power of their wounded athletes to make that balance work- and the teamwork end of the balance did not have that talent to fill in the gaps in their effectiveness. Minnesota however relied on modern tactics of teamwork without individualism and won the game.

In the final game of the month, the Storm played the Atlanta Dream on 31 May. The Storm dominated the first quarter with an eighteen to ten point lead, then entered the half with a forty-five to twenty-seven point lead. In the third quarter, the Storm led sixty-one to forty-seven and won the game with an eighty-two to sixty-five point victory. Natasha Howard led the Storm as points leader with nineteen points (roughly 1/4), and Brittney Sykes led the Dream with twelve points (roughly 1/5).

---

[23] Martin. 2019.

The game showed the need to play more than modern tactics. If every player on the team received equal possession and had the exact same amount of skill, then each player would likely receive one ninth of a team's points (roughly nine players on average play enough game time in any given game to make a significant impact in a WNBA match.) Any game where the points leader scores less that one fifth of their team's points- that player's team probably lost the game. Alternatively, any WNBA game where one athlete scores more than one third of their team's points, that team probably also lost. Finding a balance between teamwork (modernism) and individual athleticism (postmodernism) is essential for winning in the WNBA.

"Love Me Harder" Ariana Grande, The Weeknd

The Storm played four games during the first half of June. On 1 June, the team played the Chicago Sky in Chicago. Chicago took a marginal lead after the first quarter with a twenty-eight to twenty-five point lead. At the half, the Sky led the Storm forty-eight to forty-six. While remaining behind, the Storm kept the points deficit low, trailing only sixty-four to sixty-seven at the end of the third quarter. While the Storm fought hard, they could not close the points game and lost seventy-nine to eighty-three. Natasha Howard was the points leader again with twenty-one points (roughly 1/4) and Allie Quigley led the Sky with twenty five points (roughly 3/10).

After the second week of regular season games, the Storm dropped from seventh place to eighth. Ahead of the Storm were Connecticut, Minnesota, Las Vegas, Washington, Los Angeles, and Phoenix. Behind the Storm were Chicago, Atlanta, Dallas, and New York. The problem with the early rankings though is that only a shallow set of game scores determined the placement. The Storm had yet to play each other team in the league, so their position in eighth place still brought hope for finishing the season well.[24]

On 4 June, the Storm played Minnesota in Everett and dominated the first quarter twenty-five to nineteen. At half time, the Storm continued their lead forty-nine to thirty-nine. In the third quarter, Minnesota began a comeback climb to trail a single point-sixty-two to sixty-three before losing to Seattle seventy-seven to eighty-four. Jewell Loyd led the Storm as points leader with nineteen points (roughly 1/4), and Napheesa Collier led the Lynx with seventeen points (also roughly 1/4).

On 9 June, the Storm would have their chance at a rematch against Chicago in Chicago. The Sky led the first quarter twenty-nine to sixteen and ended the half with a sixty-three to forty-four point lead. In the third quarter, the Storm took the lead with a sixty-three to sixty-two point finish before losing to Chicago seventy-one to seventy-eight. Natasha Howard and Jewell Loyd shared the points

---

[24] Martin. 2019.

leader title for Seattle with twenty points each (roughly 3/10 each), and Cheyenne Parker led the Sky with eighteen points (roughly 1/4).

After the third week of games, the Storm remained in eighth place in the standings. Ahead of them were Connecticut, Washington, Los Angeles, Minnesota, Indiana, Las Vegas, and Phoenix. Behind them were Chicago, New York, Atlanta, and Dallas. Even with their defeats to Chicago, the Storm were able to keep the Sky behind them in the standings by preventing any major point deficits and performing well in other games.

On 11 June, The Storm played the Indiana Fever in Indianapolis and started the game strong. Seattle led the quarter twenty-four to seventeen. At the end of the half, Seattle led forty-six to thirty-nine. In the third quarter, Seattle continued to lead sixty-five to fifty-nine. The Fever rebounded strong, but the game ended in an eighty-four to eighty-two win for the Storm. Natasha Howard once again led the Storm as points leader with a career high of twenty-six points (roughly 3/10), while Kelsey Mitchel led the Fever with twenty-one points (roughly 1/4).

On 14 June, the Storm played the Washington Mystics in Washington DC. The Mystics led the first quarter twenty-six to twenty-four, then advanced their lead to forty-six to thirty-eight by the end of the first half. In the third quarter, Washington continued their lead to sixty-three to fifty-two before Seattle rallied to defeat Washington seventy-four to seventy-one. Natasha Howard again served as Seattle's points leader with nineteen points (roughly 1/4), and Elena Della Donne led the Mystics with equal points (also roughly 1/4).

Seattle was beginning to embrace its new, necessary tactic of adjusting their scales to adapt to the loss of Sue Bird and Breanna Stewart. As the two injured players sat out the season, they were watching their team adjust admirably. The Seattle Storm were testing whether a championship team could repeat their previous season's results under different variables- testing whether individual or team was the independent variable.

While the league's commentators were commending Connecticut for their athleticism, they also highlighted the unpredictable performance from Seattle in the absence of Bird, Stewart, and coach Hughes. In their absence, the Storm managed to establish a five to three win-loss streak going into the second half of

June. While Jonquel Jones was leading the Connecticut Sun with an average of roughly eighteen points per game, Natasha Howard was becoming the Storm's necessary warlord.[25]

"Elastic Heart" Sia

In June, the WNBA celebrated LGBTQ+ Pride Month to promote diversity and inclusion in the league in the fiftieth anniversary of the Stonewall Riots. In 1969, New York City police raided Stonewall Inn- a gay club in Greenwich Village. The raid inspired a riot among bar patrons that expanded throughout the neighborhood as a protest against police brutality and discrimination against members of the LGBT community.[26]

In 2014, the WNBA launched a website devoted to promoting the LGBT community and strengthening its partnership with their LGBTQ players and fans- becoming the first sports league to specifically market the LGBT community.[27] The move came eighteen years into the league's existence as a major step away from its ties to the conservative NBA financial base.

Even in 2019, the LGBTQ community continued to face discrimination on the bases of gender identity and sexual orientation. In fact, the most common question I received in 2019 when I told people I write books about women's sports was what my opinion was about transgender athletes in sport. (I direct them to the anthropologist's dedication to cultural relativism.)

According to the Equality Network, several sports leagues and teams continue to hesitate over action that could address homophobia and transphobia in their leagues and teams- even while acting to address concerns of other forms of discrimination over diversity. Teachers and coaches in youth and collegiate sports still waiver over intercepting the derogatory use of the term "gay" when bullies use the word against peers.[28]

Attitudes and action is changing however. Even outside of women's sports, the athletic world is embracing social activism on gender and sexuality equality. In 2019, the New York Yankees

---

[25] Martin. 2019.

[26] History.com. 2019.

[27] Murray. 2014.

[28] Equality Network. 2019.

announced their support for LGBTQ youth alongside the Boston Red Socks. Because harassment against the LGBTQ community rose following the 2016 presidential election, sports leagues across the United States felt the pressure to increase activism in support of their LGBTQ fans and players.[29]

The Seattle Storm team was an early advocate for targeting the LGBT community for mutual support. In 2001- as ticket sales were sparse- the Storm realized the potential for capitalizing on their primarily female audience. The team decided to attempt to sell tickets in bulk to lesbian organizations in the city.[30] In 2017, all five of Seattle's major sports teams- the Seahawks, Mariners, Sounders, Storm, and Reign- came together for a joint press conference over working to support Seattle's LGBTQ community.

It was the first time that the combined teams came together for a shared cause wand was a sign of changing times. While the Seahawks representatives detailed their caution over using their platform as a sports team from supporting anything too political, they shared the sentiments of the other teams over the necessity of supporting their players and their fans from discrimination.[31]

"Fearless" Jasmine Murray

The WNBA also launched an initiative in June to work towards improving mental health among their athletes. A joint partnership between the NBA and WNBA led to the development of a mobile app for meditation and mindfulness to help users improve mindset performance and better manage stress. The app included guest instruction and interviews with WNBA players Sue Bird (Seattle) and Nneka Ogwumike (Los Angeles).[32]

The announcement came at a crescendo of a season for the WNBA's collective mental health. Tensions over unreleased frustrations over financial issues, facility fallacies, and low referee quality were all taking a toll on the mental health of the league's players. During the season, the Las Vegas Aces' Liz Cambage sat out two games due to ongoing complications with depression and

---

[29] GLAAD. 2019.
[30] McCauley. 2001.
[31] Giambalvo. 2017.
[32] WNBA. 2019.

anxiety. While the NBA recently added a new rule requiring each of its league's teams have at least one mental health professional on their permanent staff; the WNBA had yet to echo the rule.[33]

The WNBA is not the only women's sports league facing a mental health crisis either. According to Vice, one third of women student-athletes in the UK face mental health problems. A 2016 study from the British Journal of Sports Medicine found roughly thirty percent of surveyed female student-athletes showed signs of depression in contrast to eighteen percent of male student-athletes.[34]

Collegiate athletes- both men and women- have the struggle of balancing schoolwork with athletics. An athlete that arrives a minute late to 6am practice as a result of staying up late to study for a test could face the punishment of not only running laps, but being responsible for her whole team running laps. The anxiety that builds from that sort of mental health environment can cause long-term mental health struggles on student-athletes. Even worse is the pressure to win. Athletes often have to sacrifice social health and personal identities to achieve the goals of the team.[35]

Part of the problem with mental health is that the symptoms are not as easy to spot as issues with physical health. While limping can be an easy mark of an athlete in need of subbing out of a game, anxiety and even eating disorders can go unseen and undiagnosed for years. University of South Carolina volleyball co-captain Victoria Garrick explained her struggle to gain body mass due to the fear of peer pressure of judgment for eating the 3000+ calorie diet necessary for maintaining such a body.

Garrick was not alone either. One in three female college athletes are at risk for an eating disorder. The combined pressure to have a body built for sport that looked (in contrast) to appear as the socially defined beauty forced Garrick into developing an eating disorder as a means of dealing with her mental struggles. Only after a two year break from volleyball and intense work with both a nutritionist and a mental health professional was the athlete able to return to her sport with a health mind and body.[36]

---

[33] Caron. 2019.
[34] Barcella. 2017.
[35] Garrick. 2017.
[36] Garrick. 2018.

Part of the mental struggle in sports goes back to the contrast of individualism and conformism- the postmodern and the modern. While every society is built on a shared world-view, the forced collective personality of a culture on its individuals can lead toward an authoritarian nightmare where individuals must sacrifice themselves to the collective desires of the tribe. Factory workers risk injury for their company for example when employers value the product more than their employees. That willingness to sacrifice the self to the tribe however only exists for as long as the individual is willing to pay that tax of personality.

Issues over that mental struggle in sport can lead to mass exodus from sport. The University of Pennsylvania's women's indoor volleyball team faced a "season of revolt" in 2019 over struggles with a rapid decline in metal health. Several veterans of the team quit mid-season, and the university cancelled the season two games early due to vulgar posters officials found in the team's locker rooms.[37]

I had some experience with mental health problems in the work place. During my time as a front desk receptionist at the Maui hostel, I struggled under mounting pressure from management to do things I was uncomfortable doing. I recall one Christmas morning where my manager yelled at me for not enforcing the "no children under six" policy when on the previous night I allowed an exception for a mother and father bringing their five-year old daughter into the hostel (on the one holiday of the year celebrating giving a family in need of travel lodging a roof to sleep under).

Eventually, the stress to conform to rules and management that I decreasingly consented to following led me to quit the job and leave for Seattle. Apparently I was not alone. In a basketball league where the top players make less money than necessary for paying year-round rent, several WNBA players spent the 2019 season venting their frustrations with poor conditions (including mental health treatment) and spoke of leaving the league altogether.

"Focus" H.E.R.

On 16 June, the Storm continued their month's games with an away match against Connecticut. Connecticut dominated the first

---

[37] Walker. 2019.

quarter with a twenty-eight to seventeen point lead. Going into the half, the Storm trailed thirty-three points to forty-four. While Seattle fought hard in the third quarter to bring the gap to a two-point difference of fifty-four to fifty-six, they could not defeat Connecticut who won the game eighty-one to sixty-seven.

Natasha Howard was the points leader for the Storm with twenty points (roughly 3/10), and Alyssa Thomas earned points leader for the Sun with equal points (roughly 1/4). After the fourth week of the regular season, the Storm rose to sixth place in the standings. Ahead of Seattle were Connecticut, Los Angeles, Las Vegas, Washington, and Chicago. Behind them were Indiana, Minnesota, Phoenix, New York, Dallas, and Atlanta.[38]

On 21 June, the Storm returned to Everett for a home game against the Sparks. Seattle led the first quarter twenty-two points to seventeen. At the end of the first half, Seattle led forty-six to thirty-four. The third quarter ended with a Seattle lead of sixty-four to forty-four before the game ended in an eighty-four to sixty-two point win for the Storm. Jewell Loyd earned the points leader award for Seattle with twenty-three points (roughly 1/4). Nneke Ogwumike earned her team's points leader award with ten points (roughly 1/6).

Two days later, the Storm played the Fever in Indianapolis. Seattle led the first quarter sixteen points to twelve before ending the first half three points behind at thirty-two points to thirty-five. The Storm continued to trail at the end of the third quarter with forty-eight points to forty-nine, but won the game with a final score of sixty-five points to sixty-one. The Storm points leader was Jewell Loyd again with twenty-one points (roughly 1/3). Erica Wheeler led the Fever with eighteen points (roughly 3/10). Following week five games, Seattle maintained its fifth spot in the rankings. Ahead of them stood Connecticut, Washington, Chicago, and Las Vegas. Behind them stood Indiana, Minnesota, Los Angeles, Phoenix, New York, Dallas, and Atlanta.[39]

On 25 June, the Storm squared off against Las Vegas in their home city. Vegas led the first quarter fifteen to nine and finished the quarter ahead of the Storm thirty-six points to thirty-two. The Aces continued their lead at the end of the third quarter forty-seven to

---

[38] Martin. 2019.
[39] Martin. 2019.

forty-three and won the game with sixty points against Seattle's fifty-six. Natasha Howard led the Storm with fourteen points (1/4) while Liz Cambage led Las Vegas with equal points (also roughly 1/4).

During the game, Jewell Loyd injured her ankle and would require at least two weeks' leave from games to heal. According to medical professionals treating the athlete, Loyd sustained a ligament sprain, bone bruise, and associated soft tissue inflammation.[40] The Storm would have to further rely on their auxiliary players as injuries mounted more than other teams as injuries continued to serve as the Storm's greatest opponent of the season.

Three days later, the Storm played the Chicago Sky at UW in Seattle. Seattle led the first quarter thirty-three points to twenty-one, then continued their lead into the half with fifty-one points to forty-three. At the end of the third quarter, the Storm led by only one point with a sixty-six to sixty-five point lead, but continued their lead with a game win of seventy-nine to seventy-six. Jordin Canada led the Storm with seventeen points (roughly 1/5), and Diamond DeShields led Chicago with nineteen points (1/4).

On the final day of June, the Storm played Phoenix in Seattle at UW. The Mercury led the first quarter nineteen points to twelve and held on to their lead at the half with thirty-four points to thirty-three. Though the Storm fought hard, Phoenix maintained their lead in the third quarter with fifty-one points to forty-eight before defeating Seattle sixty-nine points to sixty-seven.

Sami Whitcomb led the Storm as points leader with thirteen points (roughly 1/5). Brittney Griner and DeWanna Bonner shared the points leader title with twenty points each (roughly 3/10 each). Seattle managed to climb to a season high fourth place in the standings after week six games. Ahead of them stood Washington, Connecticut, and Las Vegas. Behind them stood Los Angeles, Minnesota, Phoenix, Chicago, New York, Dallas, Indiana, and Atlanta.[41]

---

[40] Voepel. 2019.
[41] Martin. 2019.

Chapter 3: Second Quarter

"Hands to Myself" Selena Gomez

On 3 July, the Storm played the New York Liberty in Seattle. The game was tied at the end of the first quarter at eighteen to eighteen. New York pulled ahead by the end of the half to lead forty-one to forty. In the third quarter however, Seattle pulled ahead to make it a seventy to sixty point game. The Storm could not hold their lead however, and the Liberty won eighty-four to eighty-three. The Storm points leader was Mercedes Russell with nineteen points (roughly 1/4), and Tina Charles led the Liberty with twenty-six points (roughly 3/10).

Two days later, the Storm played another game in Seattle against the Atlanta Dream. Atlanta led the first quarter fifteen points to thirteen and maintained their lead at the half with thirty-two points to twenty-four. The Dream continued to lead in the third quarter with fifty-six points to thirty-eight before defeating Seattle seventy-seven points to sixty-six. Natasha Howard led the Storm in their defeat with twenty points (roughly 3/10) while Tiffany Hayes led the Dream with twenty-one points (roughly 1/4). Following week seven games, the Storm fell to sixth place. Ahead of Seattle stood Washington, Las Vegas, Connecticut, Minnesota, and Los Angeles. Behind them were Phoenix, Chicago, New York, Indiana, Dallas, and Atlanta.[42]

On 12 July, Seattle played another home game against the Dallas Wings. After the first quarter, the Storm led thirty-three points to thirteen. At the end of the half, Seattle led fifty-nine points to twenty-nine. In the third quarter, the Storm led seventy-eight points to fifty-three before defeating Dallas in a final score of ninety-five to eighty-one. Kaleena Masqueda-Lewis led the Storm with eighteen points (roughly 1/5), and Arike Ogunbowale led the Wings with twenty-three points (roughly 3/10).

The prolonged break from play for Dan Hughes and Sue Bird was causing the two to find new ways to lead their team. As Dan Hughes filtered back into his coaching position, he sat down for an interview with LaChina Robinson to discuss women's basketball.

---

[42] Martin. 2019.

Hughes discussed the relationship between the WNBA and NCAA (collegiate) basketball and discussed his temporary role as an unofficial scout for the Storm. Because of Hughes' cancer treatments, he had to take a temporary role away from the court and used that time to research NCAA players.[43]

NCAA women's basketball is not far from professional. The 2019 season attracted a record setting post-season with an average of more than twenty thousand attendees for semi final and championship matches. The televised championship drew in 3.6 million viewers, which rose to 5.6 million in the final minutes of the game. These records were part of a growing trend in the popularity of women's college basketball.[44] In contrast, the WNBA five-game championship series for 2019 averaged less than half a million viewers in a twenty-one percent decline from the previous year. It was the least watch WNBA finals since 2013.[45]

Sue Bird also sat down with LaChina Robinson for an interview, but discussed her off-the court roles as an injured veteran. For years, Sue Bird hosted a satirical interview show with other basketball players (and occasionally other athletes) in a series called "Between Two Birds." (This is a reference to another satirical interview show called "Between Two Ferns" with host Zach Galifianakis.) Bird also discussed NCAA basketball and detailed the changing times caused by a combination of changes in recruiting processes and coaching staff.

"Between Two Birds" is a perfect example of the need for individualism in the WNBA. Like with Seattle Reign's 2017 Haley Kopmeyer's "Stops with Kop,"- a YouTube series which spotlighting soccer players traveling around Seattle with Kopmeyer and interviewing each other about the team- Sue Bird's series helps lend humanity to the athletes that play in the WNBA. Bird's series helps fans of the league learn more about players and introduces off-the-court personalities to fans who may only know athletes as members of a team.

Sue Bird also discussed the changing times of the WNBA. Bird discussed standout draft players before explaining one major

---

[43] Robinson 2019.

[44] Durham. 2019.

[45] Sports Media Watch. 2019.

change in the draft. In the past, there was typically one draft option that stood high above the others, but the 2019 season saw several highly and equally qualified players join the league. This is likely a result of the success of the NCAA, and could be a sign for improved ratings and viewership in the WNBA. Bird also explained the mental and physical needs of athletes, and how younger players tend to rely on physical fitness while older players rely on mental fitness.[46]

On 14 July, the Storm played the Liberty again in Seattle. The Storm led the first quarter twenty-seven to twenty, then ended the half with a forty-three to thirty point lead. At the end of the third quarter, Seattle led sixty-six points to forty-three before winning the game seventy-eight to sixty-nine. Crystal Langhorne led the Storm with nineteen points (roughly 1/4), and Kia Nurse led New York with equal points (also roughly 1/4).

Following week eight games, Seattle held onto its number six spot in the standings. Ahead of the Storm were Las Vegas, Connecticut, Washington, Minnesota, and Los Angeles. Behind them were Chicago, Phoenix, New York, Atlanta, Indiana, and Dallas.[47] With the season approaching its midway point, the team standings were beginning to coagulate into a form that reflected their overall.

"Warrior (Battle Cry Remix)" Hannah Kerr

Basketball is a team sport- but the small team sizes emphasize the effect of each individual player. As five players are on the court at one time, it is not unheard of for a single player to score more than the team's points-per-player average. Like any given small-group population, the survival of the group depends on the skills of the individual. But while the strengths of the individual are essential for the success of the group, an overabundance of individualism on the part of an athlete in a team sport can equally cause problems.

The soul of individualism is the definition of a person's identity. That identity consists of the basic values that dictate the choices an individual makes. These basic values often take from the experiences an individual has endured over their life combined with

---

[46] Robinson. 2019.
[47] Martin 2019.

the way in which they react to the environment and events around them. A person's roles and responsibilities can also affect their identity. Someone who is a teacher, a father, and a friend may have separate responsibilities for each role that can influence the decisions the individual makes.[48]

For athletes, athletic identity can sometimes work against them. Athletes often tie their identity to their achievements. A championship basketball player for example might define their identity with their success as an athlete. In fencing, gold-medal athletes often retire from the sport as soon as they start performing worse than they could- believing they had already reached their "peak" and want to retire before their winning record diminishes.

A further level of identity comes from their fame. As the majority of people who know the athletes know them for their athletic achievements, those people will identify them by those athletic achievements. For example, the vast majority of people who know who Michael Jordan is would know him for his athletic performance as a basketball player, but few would know him for his role as a father or a husband or a son. This can then be an issue for an athlete following retirement because the person can feel like they are performing a role they do no fit into.[49]

Imagine for a moment an actor who played a character in a TV show for years- say ten years. Now imagine that actor leaving the show to go perform a role in a new show. It is often hard for audiences to un-see the role that actor played in the past while the actor plays their new role. That audience reaction to the new role can affect the actor's confidence in their new role. With athletes, this can cause an identity crisis when they leave sports to begin new, post-retirement roles.

Even short-term departures from playing sports can affect an athlete's sense of self. An injury that causes an athlete to miss an entire season can cause long-term effects on the athlete's confidence. Young athletes that leave sports can also find difficulty in discovering new identities. I had an interesting conversation with my manager at the hostel I worked at in Seattle one day about this latter issue.

---

[48] Heshmat. 2014.
[49] Lemmons. 2019.

Collegiate athletes spend a massive amount of their time in college either practicing for or competing in their respective sports-which can take away time from their education, but it is still imperative that the athlete study something while at school. If not, college would be more comparable to a trade school where say an electrician earns their certification through hands-on training to become a skilled worker.

The problem with that model for sports though is that athletes are rarely able to be competitive athletes until aged sixty-five. Eventually, an athlete must retire from their sport and get a new job. Having a college degree in economics, anthropology, or cinematography (or really any field) can help prepare an athlete for their inevitable metamorphosis away from their role as a professional athlete.

This is especially important for women athletes. While some male athletes make enough money during their time in competition to save enough money to last throughout their athletic retirement, few women athletes make enough money during their time as professionals to last the rest of their life. Another layer that creates difficulty for athletes in establishing a post-athletic identity is the "looking-glass self."

The looking-glass self is the way in which an individual judges themselves through the observation of others. This could include a person hearing someone call them "fat" suddenly feeling like they need to lose weight. When it comes to athletes, hearing their identity being tied to their role as a "soccer player" or a "surfer" can cause a crisis when that identifying title no longer applies. (Who is Michael Jordan if not a basketball player?) No matter how individualistic a person might be, a person's identity is still partially shaped by what and who society wants the person to be.[50]

This is where the balance between individualism and conformity become essential. Take college-level women's basketball. While each athlete on a team must perform the personality their coach(es) need them to perform on the court, each athlete must simultaneously perform a chosen role outside of the arena in the classroom as a student of a field of their own choosing.

---

[50] Lesley University. 2019.

If that student-athlete then becomes a professional athlete, they must maintain that secondary potential career option as a postmodern choice while performing the modern role their coach(es) assign for them on the court. Even then however, the individual will leave basketball and join a workforce where their manager or boss will need the former athlete to perform a role of the manager's choosing, and the cycle of balancing modernism and postmodernism continues.

"Sit Still, Look Pretty" Daya, R!OT

Once a given culture or subculture establishes a sense of "looking-glass self" in an individual, that individual becomes susceptible to socialization- the process by which a culture or subculture trains an individual into becoming the person that culture wants the person to become. Socialization is not inherently good or bad. A child is socialized into learning how to use a toilet at an early age by parents or caretakers so that they don't need to wear a diaper for their entire life, and reverent individuals often undergo sacramental coming-of-age rituals to earn their status as adults in their given faith.

In sports, socialization can establish an athlete's role on their team and in the sport. More importantly, the lessons and character traits an athlete earns while participating in sports can carry over to lead to success in fields outside of sports. According to the Women's Sports Foundation; girls that play sports in high school are less likely to be involved in unplanned pregnancy, more likely to get higher grades in school, and are more likely to graduate than non-athlete peers. Athletic girls on average display higher confidence and lower levels of depression, and have greater overall body image.[51]

Socialization into the WNBA however does not always have beneficial effects on its players. In 2018, sports in the United States had a clear hierarchy. Admittedly, this is not just in basketball. Some men's sports are deemed more important than other men's sports. In a country where baseball and football dominate, even men's soccer struggles to gain the same attendance and television airtime as the NFL. When it comes to the gender divide in US sports however,

---

[51] Women's Sports Foundation. 2016.

there is a clear dominant half- and even the WNBA was struggling to remain unbiased.

In 2017, the Minnesota Lynx had to surrender their "home court advantage" (a term often used to describe a team's greater odds of victory while playing on the court they play on for home games) to play in St. Paul's Xcel Energy Center while their usual home court was under renovation for the local NHL team. The four-time WNBA championship team was relegated to a downgraded stadium because a men's league of a completely different sport needed their stadium. This is exactly what happened to the Seattle Storm in 2019.

A men's sports team would never be asked to play in a different stadium for an entire season to accommodate renovations to a stadium for a women's sports team. That clear bias towards favoring men's sports creates a sense of secondary status for women that women have far too long had to endure. When the WNBA league and team officials agree to decisions like that, they make the choice to socialize their players into accepting that men matter more than women- and by 2019, the athletes of the WNBA were ready to challenge that philosophy.

The issues did not stop at facility substitution either. The WNBA forced the Las Vegas Aces to forfeit a 2018 game the Aces refused to play out of travel fatigue. Forced to travel for twenty-five straight hours without sleep to reach Washington DC for a game in the 2018 season, the Aces refused to play a game out of a collective decision that rest was more important than the risk of injuries that could occur as a result of their travel complications. The league told the Aces the result would be an automatic loss- a move the NBA would never do.

While men in sports enjoy greater power as individuals, women in sports enjoy no individual power. From this approach, the WNBA established a culture where their players do not matter, and only the league had any significant decision making power. While the NBA usually stands by its players for standing up as individuals in protest against social issues, the WNBA often punishes its players for being social activists. While male athletes often protest against societal wrongs (such as racial discrimination), women in the WNBA have historically received fines for minor acts like wearing black warm-up t-shirts in quiet protest against discrimination.[52]

This comes after already receiving salaries so low that most WNBA players receive pay lower than the equivalent monetary value of their scholarship to universities where they played NCAA basketball. When benefits, scholarships, and pay are figured into the equation of pay women basketball players receive, most collegiate players are treated better than professionals. It's no wonder then why frustration was building in the WNBA as players found themselves designated not only secondary to men or to other sports, but to their own past selves.

"Issues" Julia Michaels

On 17 July, the Storm met the Lynx in Minnesota for their next game. Seattle dominated the first quarter with twenty-six points to sixteen, then ended the half fifty points to forty. In the third quarter, the Storm led the game with seventy-one points to fifty-four before winning the game with ninety points against Minnesota's seventy-nine. Natasha Howard led the Storms with thirty-three points (more than 1/3) while Lexie Brown led the Lynx with twenty points (roughly 1/4).

On 19 July, the Storm headed back to UW to compete against Las Vegas in Seattle. The Storm led the first quarter twenty-one to thirteen, then ended the first half forty-three to thirty-five. Seattle continued to lead in the third quarter with fifty-five points to sixty-nine before winning the game in a close sixty-nine points to the Aces' sixty-six. Natasha Howard led the Storm once again with twenty-one points (roughly 3/10), and Liz Cambage led the Aces with sixteen points (roughly 1/4). Seattle found itself in fourth place in the league standings following week nine games. Ahead of them stood Las Vegas, Washington, and Connecticut. Behind them stood Chicago, Los Angeles, Minnesota, Phoenix, New York, Indiana, Dallas, and Atlanta.[53]

On 23 July, the Aces had their chance at a rematch in Las Vegas. Seattle barely led the first quarter with twenty-one points to twenty, but the Aces led the first half with thirty-six points to thirty-five. Las Vegas held their lead by finishing the third quarter fifty-five to forty-eight, then defeated the Storm in a final score of

---

[52] Blackistone. 2018.
[53] Martin 2019.

seventy-nine to sixty-two. Dearica Hamby led the Aces with twenty-four points (roughly 3/10), and Natasha Howard and Alysha Clark tied as the Storm points leaders with thirteen points (roughly 1/5) each.

At about the same time, the WNBA was preparing for its All-Star game- an exhibition match that would pit the best players from across the league against each other in two teams. Each team would consist of five starting players and five reserve players. Two Seattle Storm players made the roster as starters- Natasha Howard and Jewell Loyd. No Storm players made the reserve roster.[54]

On the 27 July All-Star game, Elena Della Donne led her team- including Jewell Loyd) against Aja Wilson's team under Napheesa Collier's leadership (due to Wilson being out on injury)- including Natasha Howard. Team Delle Donne trailed in the first quarter twenty-three points to Wilson's thirty-nine. Wilson's team led the half with seventy-seven points to sixty-three. In the third quarter, Wilson's team led one hundred five to ninety-five before winning one hundred twenty-nine points to one hundred twenty-six.

Nneka Ogwumike led Team Delle Donne as points leader with twenty-two points (roughly 1/6), and Erica Wheeler led Team Wilson with twenty-five points (roughly 1/5). Following week ten games, the Storm dropped to fifth place in the standings. Ahead of them were Las Vegas, Washington, Connecticut, and Chicago. Behind them stood Los Angeles, Phoenix, Minnesota, New York, Indiana, Dallas, and Atlanta.[55]

---

[54] Martin 2019.
[55] Martin 2019.

"Starships" Nicki Minaj

On 2 August, the Storm played the Washington Mysics in Seattle at the university stadium. Washington led the first quarter with twenty-three points to twelve before leading the half with forty-eight points to Seattle's thirty-four. Washington continued to lead the game in the third quarter with seventy-eight points to sixty before winning the game ninety-nine to seventy-nine. Natasha Howard led the Storm as points leader with twenty-six points (roughly 1/3), and Elena Della Donne led the Mystics with twenty-nine points (roughly 3/10).

Seattle headed to Los Angeles for their next game against the Sparks on 4 August. The Sparks led the first quarter twenty-seven to twenty-four before leading the first half with fifty points to forty-one. Los Angeles led the third quarter with fifty-six points to fifty before winning the game eighty-three to seventy-five. Seattle's third quarter defense was not enough to save it from defeat in the game.

Alysha Clark and Sami Whitcomb tied as points leaders for the Storm with sixteen points (roughly 1/5) each, and Candace Parker led the Sparks with twenty-one points (roughly 1/4). Following week eleven games, the Storm fell to seventh place in the standings. Ahead of them stood Connecticut, Washington, Las Vegas, Los Angeles, Chicago, and Phoenix. Behind them stood Minnesota, Indiana, New York, Dallas, and Atlanta.[56]

On 8 August, the Storm headed back to Seattle to play the Dallas Wings at their university stadium. Dallas led the first quarter twenty-four points to twenty, then barely held their lead at the end of the half with a thirty-eight to thirty-seven point lead. Seattle took the lead in the third quarter with fifty-two points to Dallas' forty-seven before winning the game sixty-nine to fifty-seven. Natasha Howard led the Storm with twenty-three points (1/3), and Kayla Thornton led the Wings with fourteen points (roughly 1/4).

On 11 August, the Storm headed to New York City to play the Liberty. Seattle led the first quarter twenty-three to seventeen, but New York took the lead to end the first half forty-five to forty-

---

[56] Martin 2019.

three. Seattle regained the lead to end the third quarter seventy to fifty-seven before winning the game eighty-four to sixty-nine. Alysha Clark led the Storm as their points leader with twenty-one points (1/4) while Tina Charles led the Liberty with twenty-two points (roughly 1/3).

Elsewhere in the league, two other teams made infamous news. During a game between Phoenix and Dallas, a fight erupted between players on the court in response to a referee call on the floor. Halfway into the fourth quarter, Brittney Griner was attempting to block a shot from a Dallas player when their arms got tangled in mid-air under the basket. Tempers flared, and Griner charged the Dallas player- even attempting to overpower a referee trying to break up the pursuit.

Several other players became involved in an attempt to both support their own team members and to hold back opposing players in what became the biggest fight in the WNBA since a 2008 fight between players from Los Angeles and Detroit. Five total players from the 2019 fight received suspensions for their involvement, and three players received five hundred dollar fines.[57]

Following week twelve games, Seattle recovered slightly to move into the sixth spot in the standings. Ahead of the Storm stood Washington, Los Angeles, Las Vegas, Connecticut, and Chicago. Behind the Storm stood Minnesota, Phoenix, Indiana, New York, Dallas, and Atlanta.[58] In order for the Storm to make the postseason, they would need to finish no worse than eighth place, which meant they would need to maintain their record to prevent themselves from losing the opportunity to enter the approaching post-season.

On 14 August, the Storm played the Mystics once again in Washington DC. Seattle led the first quarter twenty-three to sixteen before Washington took the lead to end the half thirty-eight to thirty-five. The Mystics held their lead to end the third quarter fifty-nine to fifty-one before crushing the Storm in a final score of eighty-eight to fifty-nine. Natasha Howard led the Storm with twenty-four points (2/5) while Aerial Powers led the Mystics with sixteen points (less than 1/5).

---

[57] ESPN. 2019.
[58] Brian. 2019.

"Roar" Katy Perry

The mental fatigue of travel, pay, and facility quality woes paired with a rising epidemic in women's sports- including in the WNBA. As I discovered while researching the USWNT in Behind the Goal (available in paperback!), women athletes often feel the need to overexert themselves to achieve still a fraction of the attention male athletes receive. While male basketball players can afford to flop on the court, athletes in the WNBA- like in women's soccer- often must endure physical pain and fouls to be taken seriously as athletes.

This is also not just an issue in sports. Women who report pain to medical professionals often find disbelief. Even trained medical doctors often tell women patients that the patient is exaggerating their pain. This is especially hard on women of color. In his show "Last Week Tonight," host John Oliver explored the medical bias in the United States against women and people of color in a medical profession designed towards treating white men.

Examples from the show's episode on medical bias included a study that showed women are less likely to be referred for a knee replacement than a man, women over fifty were less likely to receive life-saving interventions, and were less likely to receive any pain medicine for abdominal pains reported in emergency room visits. Medically, female homo sapiens actually show different symptoms to certain medical emergencies than their male counterparts- including heart attacks. Because medical professionals are only trained in spotting the male signs of a heart attack however, many women enduring a heart attack are often denied emergency medical aid.

Among African-Americans, the bias against them in American medicine can have lethal effects. African-American patents are less likely to receive medical coverage for treatment for pneumonia, hip fractures, and several types of cancer including breast, lung, and prostate cancer. Part of the problem is that medical students in 2016 discovered most medical research around African-Americans was embarrassingly incorrect. This included twenty-five percent of medical residents incorrectly believing that African-Americans had thicker skin than their white peers.[59]

---

[59] Oliver. 2019.

Within the sports community, those biases against women and people of color extend to athletes. To make things even worse, there is little discussion about sports injuries and pain; which makes athletes feel like they cannot openly talk about their pain without judgment. Another major problem is the very nature of how sports work in the United States. Most modern American sports (soccer and basketball included) derive from sports invented with male athletes in mind- and there are clear biological differences between male and female homo sapiens.

While the anatomies of human beings are greatly unique to the individual, there is clear sexual dimorphism in human bone structure and muscles. Over three million years of human evolution, male and female bodies evolved for vastly different activities. While male bodies evolved for short and medium length tests of endurance, female bodies evolved to endure long-term stress (which is part of the reason why female bodies require more time to lose body fat than males of the species). Because most sports were invented with male athletes in mind (like basketball), the way male and female athletes play in those sport have to be different.

According to author Michael Sokolove, female athletes who play sports designed for male anatomy over a prolonged period of time can cause serious injuries to the athlete's body. Women are also under a secondary societal demand in the United States to fit into the mold of beauty that American culture created around ideas of what the body looks like more than what the body is capable of. The struggle of attempting to create two different anatomies in a single body can cause intense injuries in women athletes.

To make matters even more difficult, pay inequality between women and men athletes is so dramatic, that most professional women's sports leagues pay women athletes below the poverty level. Because of the impossibly low pay, most women athletes have to compete in year-round play (like basketball players who play in other leagues overseas)- denying their bodies from recovery time and increasing the odds of sustaining injuries.[60]

There is no wonder then why so many players in the WNBA have built up frustration. The athletes compete in a country whose doctors do not take their pain seriously, for a coaches that pushes

---

[60] Sokolove. 2008.

them beyond what their bodies spent three million years evolving to do, and a league that pays them so low that they are forced to double the odds of sustaining long-term injury- and those are only issues affecting their physical health.

"Tightrope" Janelle Monae, Big Boi

Quality refereeing has long plagued the sports world- regardless of the gender of the athletes. As a competitive fencer, I learned all about refereeing before contemporary technology. Before fencing began integrating electronic technology into its scoring system, referees made decisions in what was known as a bout committee. In each bout between two athletes, a central referee stood at the centerline outside of the piste (the strip of ground fencers compete on). One referee stood also at each of the four corners of the piste. When the central referee saw what they believed to be one fencer touching the other fencer with his/her sword; the play paused, and the referees voted on the outcome.

Technology has greatly improved fencing scoring now- giving referees the ability to use video assistance for reviewing challenges to their decisions. Technology however cannot solve every problem in refereeing. Low-quality refereeing caused significant outcomes in the 2015 Women's World Cup in Canada where the New Zealand team failed to advance into the knockout stage because of a wrongful call over a handball incident that never actually occurred.[61]

The fault with the all-women referee team in the 2015 Women's World Cup was not the gender of the referees, but the gender of the predecessors. Because the 2015 world cup was the first to require only women referees, those officiating the games did not have very much experience- leading to a small number (but significant in importance) of bad calls. With more women referees with as much experience as men, referees with empathy and understanding of the needs of women athletes will have greater odds of making correct calls during games.[62]

Psychologically, the struggle for equal refereeing goes beyond sports. According to Psychology Today, referees make

---

[61] Kargraf. 2015.
[62] Kirpalani. 2018.

harsher judgments of women athletes than men athletes in the same sport. In a study examining refereeing in Division 1 handball in France, researchers found referees far more harshly disciplined women handball players than men handball players for the same transgressions. The researches believed this derived from referees believing women athletes should be less aggressive than men athletes.[63]

In 2016, the Minnesota Lynx lost their championship game as a result of what several journalists claim to have been a poor referee call late in the game. In game four of the championship series, referees refused to call a penalty on a timing violation which went on to give the Los Angeles Sparks a lead in the fourth quarter and a championship win for the season.[64]

Referee quality in the WNBA has not changed much since 2016. In what would be the Chicago Sky's final game of the 2019 season, referees ejected player Astou Ndour for a foul against a referee. While sitting on the bench following an early-game technical foul, Ndour reached out her arm to show a referee proof of another player's fouling of fellow player Cheyenne Parker when the referee- not looking at Ndor- walked into her arm. The referee instantly ejected Ndour for assaulting him, and all other referees (all men) agreed to the ejection following a review of the call.[65]

Even when there is clear gender discrimination against women in sport, their reasonable complaints often fall on deaf ears. This is not just a problem with refereeing either. Numerous cases of reports of gender discrimination and sexual harassment find no follow-ups and mostly male administrators choose to believe their fellow male peers over their female athletes- including historically USA Gymnastics and USA Swimming.

Women athletes in the United States are simply not taken seriously as athletes, and to make problems worse for the WNBA- there are places in the world where they are taken seriously. WNBA players make on average one fifth of the salary of NBA players- with a WNBA pay cap of $110K, but pay in Europe is far greater. Median salaries in the WNBA rest at about $50K while the EuroLeague

---

[63] Bruggen & Persaud. 2018.
[64] Borzi. 2016.
[65] Kenney. 2019.

starting salaries rest at twice that value. The lowest paid EuroLeague players earn what the highest paid WNBA players make.[66]

Not only is the pay in the United States lower, but the purchasing power of that pay is lower too. The cost of living in the United States has started a housing crisis across the country. In Seattle, the average cost of rent for an average sized apartment (696 square feet) in Seattle is two thousand one hundred dollars per month as of 2019.[67] Of the cheapest eleven cities in the United States, only one had a WNBA team- Las Vegas- where the rent average for an average size apartment (894 square feet) is eleven hundred dollars per month.[68]

In Ekaterinburg, Russia- home of the EuroLeague team UMCC Ekaterinburg- rent for the average apartment (roughly 900 square feet) cost roughly $450 US per month in 2019.[69] In Lyon, France- the most expensive city with a EuroLeague team in 2019- the average cost of rent for an average sized apartment (900 square feet) was roughly $1000 US per month in 2019.[70] Women are paid far more in Europe for playing basketball and the most expensive city in the league to live in is still cheaper than the cheapest US WNBA city to live in.

As games continued into the second half of August, I started wondering why any of the WNBA players continue to play in a league that continuously devalues them, underpays them, and provides poor refereeing- and I was not the only one. Several players in the league were reaching a boiling point with serious consideration for leaving the league for good. The 2019 WNBA season threatened to be the proverbial high water mark ahead of what could be the eventual end of the league.

"End Game" Taylor Swift, Ed Sheeran, Future
On 16 August, the Storm met the Sun for a game in Connecticut. The Sun led the first quarter twenty-one to seventeen, but the Storm rallied to lead the first half forty-six points to thirty-

---

[66] Lamonier. 2018.
[67] Rent Cafe. 2019.
[68] Rent Cafe. 2019.
[69] Expatistan. 2019.
[70] Expatistan. 2019.

four. The Storm maintained their lead in the third quarter with sixty-three points to fifty-eight, but the Sun counter-attacked and ended the game with a thrilling win with seventy-nine points over Seattle's seventy-eight. Natasha Howard led the Storm as points leader with twenty-seven points (more than 1/3) while Shekinna Stricklen led the Sun with twenty-four points (roughly 3/10).

On Sunday, 18 August; I headed to the UW home for the Storm for a game against the Minnesota Lynx. It would be the only live game I was able to attend in person, and I powerfully empathized with players during the game. During the entire time I was in Seattle, I depended on help from friends and family just to pay my bills. I was relying on crowdfunding to fund my research-something I never had to do in the past at such a degree as in this study. As I purchased my ticket with the last twenty-five dollars in my bank account for the month, I wondered how players in the league survived on their pay.

I entered the stadium, found my seat- one of the cheapest available- and sat down among a roughly seventy-five percent attendance. Following the first quarter, Seattle led twenty-one to fourteen, then continued their lead into half time with forty-eight points to thirty-nine. During the third quarter, Seattle continued their lead with sixty-seven points to sixty-three before winning the game eighty-two to seventy-four. Jordin Canada led the Storm with fourteen points (roughly 1/6) while Odysseey Sims led the Lynx with thirty points (roughly 2/5).

After the game, I spoke with some of the Storm fans on our way to the bus stop. They were proud of the Storm's win and talked about how much Jordin Canada's performance impressed them. They also talked about knowing Sami Whitcomb's aunt and about how the game was the first time they were able to see a game live. Then they hopped on their bus as I continued to wait for mine.

Following week thirteen games, the Seattle Storm rested in sixth place. Teams ahead of them in the standings were Washington, Connecticut, Las Vegas, Los Angeles, and Chicago. Teams behind Seattle in the standings were Phoenix, Minnesota, Dallas, Indiana, New York, and Atlanta.[71] On 23 August, The Seattle met the Indiana Fever in Seattle for their next game.

---

[71] Martin 2019.

Indiana led the first quarter with an eighteen to fourteen point lead and maintained their lead with thirty-three points to Seattle's twenty-six at the half. Indiana continued their lead in the third quarter with fifty-one points to Seattle's thirty-nine before defeating the Storm in a final score of sixty-three to fifty-four. Natasha Howard led the Storm with fourteen points (roughly 1/4), and Teaira McCowan led the Fever with twenty-two points (more than 1/3).

Following week fourteen games, the Storm maintained their sixth spot in the standings. Ahead of them stood Washington, Los Angeles, Connecticut, Chicago, and Las Vegas. Behind Seattle stood Minnesota, Phoenix, Indiana, Dallas, New York, and Atlanta.[72] For their last game of the month, Seattle played the Connecticut Sun in Seattle on 27 August.

Connecticut led the first quarter with twenty-four points to Seattle's twenty. The Sun continued to lead with forty-four points to thirty-six at the half. In the third quarter, Connecticut took a commanding lead of seventy-one points to forty-nine before winning the game in a final score of eighty-nine to seventy. Jewell Loyd led the Storm with eighteen points (roughly 1/4), and Alyssa Thomas led the Sun with twenty-two points (also roughly 1/4).

---

[72] Martin 2019.

"Hold My Hand" Jess Glynne

On 1 September, the Seattle Storm played their next game in their quest to enter the postseason against Atlanta in Seattle. Seattle dominated the first quarter with twenty-eight points to sixteen and continued their lead into the half with fifty-three to thirty-six. The Storm maintained their lead in the third quarter with sixty-nine to fifty-five before winning the game ninety-two to seventy-five.

Jordin Canada led the Storm with twenty-one points (roughly 1/4), and Renee Montgomery and Monique Billings tied as the points leaders for Atlanta with fifteen points (1/5) each. After week fifteen games, Seattle dropped to seventh place in the standings. Ahead of them stood Washington, Connecticut, Los Angeles, Las Vegas, Chicago, and Minnesota. Behind them stood Phoenix, Indiana, Dallas, New York, and Atlanta.[73]

On 3 September, the Storm met the Mercury for a game in Phoenix and started the game strong with a twenty-five to eighteen point lead in the first quarter. Going into halftime, the Storm maintained their lead with fifty points to Phoenix's thirty-five. In the third quarter, the Storm led seventy-two to fifty-two before winning the game eighty-two to seventy. Natasha Howard led the Storm with twenty-two points (roughly 1/4), and Brittney Griner led the Mercury with equal points (roughly 3/10).

On 5 September, Seattle played the Sparks in Los Angeles. The Sparks led the first quarter with twenty-five points to nineteen before ending the half with a fifty to thirty-five point lead. In the third quarter, the Sparks continued their lead with seventy-six points to fifty-one before defeating Seattle in a final score of one hundred eight to sixty-eight. Natasha Howard and Jewell Loyd led the Storm with thirteen points (roughly 1/5) each, and Candace Parker led the Sparks with twenty points (roughly 1/6).

On 8 September, the Storm played their last regular season game against the Wings in Dallas. The Storm ended the first quarter with a twenty-four to fourteen point lead before ending the half with forty-four points to thirty-six. In the third quarter, the Storm led

---

[73] Martin 2019.

sixty-two to fifty before ending the game in a seventy-eight to sixty-four point win. Natasha Howard led the Storm with twenty-two points (roughly 3/10), and Arike Ogunbowale led the Wings with twenty-five points (roughly 2/5). The Storm's victory paved their way into the postseason.

In a new set-up for the postseason, the WNBA would host a wild card round where the lowest four teams would compete for wild card entry into the bracket (similar to Major League Baseball), and the top two teams would get a double by into the semifinals. The wild card winners would compete in the quarterfinals against places three and four to decide the other two teams of the semifinals.[74]

"Hollow" Tori Kelly, Big Sean

One of the biggest questions I had throughout my study was why WNBA players were paid so little. Even when compared to other women basketball players, the WNBA athletes were barely paid anything compared to their relatively unheard of EuroLeague peers. There had to be some reason for why the highest paid WNBA players were still paid less than EuroLeague athletes. My first attempt to find an answer was to look at league sponsors. League and team sponsorships provide a major influence on pay for athletes.

Major sponsors for the WNBA included for the 2019 season AT&T, Adidas, American Express, Budweiser, Gatorade, Spalding, and Nike- just to name a few.[75] On the EuroLeague's women's basketball list of sponsors, I had never heard of any of their long list of names. Next I thought it could be ticket sales. Perhaps- somehow- the EuroLeague was able to bring in more fans to watch women's basketball games.

The average attendance for a WNBA game in 2018 was about 6800 attendees at an average ticket price of about $17.50 per ticket.[76] In a comparative women's basketball league in Australia- where some WNBA players go to play in the offseason- pay is less than the WNBA's. The base minimum salary for women in Australia's basketball league is $13K per year.[77] That might seem

---

[74] Robinson. 2019.

[75] WNBA. 2019.

[76] Jope. 2019.

[77] Uluc. 2019.

low, but the average attendance per home game for one team- the 2019 champions Canberra Capitals- was 1200 attendees for the season.[78] That's an average minimum pay of eleven dollars per ticket sale.

If the WNBA's more famous basketball players are making an average of less than $72K per year at an average of 6800 fans per game, then they are making less money per ticket sold than the Australian women, less overall pay than European women, and spend more money on living expenses than either. The secret spending in the WNBA limiting its ability to pay its players is in variables other leagues don't have to deal with- healthcare and retirement.

Healthcare in the United States is one of the most expensive in the world, and the teams of the WNBA ensure all of their players while teams abroad often do not. Also, the WNBA provides retirement benefits to players that foreign teams do not provide, nor do other leagues provide dependable paychecks. In several different sports, American athletes in Russian sports leagues reported never receiving the promised pay.[79]

For Seattle Storm's Sue Bird and Phoenix Mercury's Diana Turasi, that experience playing in Russia was not only strange for the difference in payout and dependability of pay, but for another variable non-existent in the United States- espionage. In a 2019 documentary, the two WNBA players spoke about a former coach they had while playing basketball in Russia. Coach Shabtai Kalmanovich was well known for spoiling his star players- providing the type of pay, travel, lodging, and benefits that most players in the NBA receive. Their coach however was a double agent spy with mob connections who used illicit funds to pay for his basketball team.[80]

While obviously not every women's sports team outside of the United States is practicing shady business models, the women's sports leagues in the US are under far stricter regulations and have hidden fees they pay athletes beyond other leagues' teams. With all that being said, there is still the trouble of why athletes in the WNBA

---

[78] Helmers. 2019.
[79] Voepel. 2018.
[80] ESPN. 2019.

are paid so little. Perhaps the athletes' pay truly is tied to attendance. Perhaps the biggest problem is neither sponsor nor league- but fans.

With an average attendance of about 6800 per game, adding a new team to the league would not increase profits for the league. Getting more fans for the already established teams is what is needed to increase revenue and therefore increase pay. The next question then is why the WNBA struggles to bring in the necessary attendance for establishing a living wage for players.

The average game attendance for the NBA in 2018 was about 18K attendees per game with an average salary of $6.4M US with an average price per ticket of $89. If the WNBA's numbers are $71.6K pay per average player divided by the average attendance per game of 6800 further divided by the average price per ticket of $17.50- then a WNBA player's pay is roughly 60% of a ticket. The same figure for NBA players is 400% the price per ticket. There's more to revenue than ticket sales though. The NBA is a highly successful sports league with highly successful individual teams that make money on far more than attendance at live games.

The men's basketball league is able to fund its expensive lodging, travel, and facility fees through a combination of ticket sales, suite sales, naming rights, and media (TV and radio) rights along with merchandise and sponsorship. There are NBA jerseys and bobble heads, broadcasting rights overseas, and exclusive seating at games. Small market teams spend nearly sixty percent of their budgets on player salaries and the other forty percent on business operating expenses, team non-staff costs, team staff costs, and a combination of other expenses.[81] Even with all that spending though, the revenue far surpasses the costs.

Unlike the WNBA, there is a huge international market for men's basketball viewership overseas. In 2019, this actually put the NBA in a difficult position as deals with broadcasting in China was rapidly leading to issues of free speech and freedom of press among both members of the league and teams and with fans attending televised live games. Because broadcasting companies across the world pay steep fees for the right to air the NBA in their respective countries, the league is able to use that money to fund the high salaries of their players.

---

[81] Wertheim. 2018.

Unfortunately, the WNBA does not have the same international appeal that the NBA has. This is not unique to basketball either. While the USWNT of US Soccer has been able to help establish a market for international women's soccer, domestic leagues- such as the NWSL in the United States or the W-League in Australia- continue to maintain televised audiences abroad. Even in their own countries, national-level leagues struggle to get television airtime.

When I first reached Seattle in March, I stayed with a Couchsurfer host who worked in the tech industry who was a huge fan of the Seattle Sounders- Seattle's men's soccer team. I asked why he believed the Sounders attracted so many fans in a sport where American women perform so intensely better than American men- and when Reign FC continued to work hard to get just a fraction of the Sounders' attendees.

The guy told me that he grew up in Boston and came to Seattle for the same reason most move to the city- for a tech job. He told me that a lot of the people in Seattle's tech industry- like himself- were born in other countries where soccer is the most popular sport. Attending soccer games helps bring a sense of home to the many Seattle tech workers who were born in countries where their men perform better than their women. This helps explain too why more people actually attend Sounders games than Seahawks games- a team of the most popular sport among Americans. The sheer volume of Seattle's immigrant population showed in sports attendance statistics.

It's hard to convince people born and raised watching men's sports and who have no access to viewing women's sports to attend women's sports games. During my time in Hawaii, I thought about this concept through the lens of linguistic relativity. Linguistic relativity is a term in anthropology that describes the relationship between how a person's experiences affect how they interpret the world around them and how a person's world-view affects their experiences. This can describe how a painter might look at a color wheel and point out more unique shades of the color blue than perhaps a park ranger. It can also extend into sports viewership.

There are far more men's sports on television than women's. As young humans watch sports on television and see far more men than women- or in some cases never seeing women athletes- that experience creates a worldview that men are supposed to be athletes and women aren't. I developed a theory that if women's sports and men's sports were aired exactly equally in every corner of the world for enough years that no one alive would have been alive during a time of airtime inequality- then women athletes would be equally respected as men athletes.

"Gonna Love Me" Teyana Taylor

The WNBA will likely never receive the spending budget or the viewership of the NBA, but men's sports are not the only sports drawing in fans and producing profitable income. Across the world, women's sports are growing in fans and revenue. In 2017, a women's Australian Rules Football league started in Australia with thunderous support. Nearly every match found sold-out seating during the opening season.

Part of that success came from making tickets temporarily free- a perfectly great reason for a person to attend a live game. That initial entrance acted as a gateway to fans of the sport becoming fans of the teams. Once a massive fan base was secure- including an audience of fifty-three thousand fans at one championship match- the teams began charging for tickets. That allowed the league to begin paying its players more than its previous minimum pay of thirty-seven thousand dollars per season.[82]

Ticket pricing is not the issue however. Tickets to WNBA games are about as cheap as the teams can afford them to be. Women's basketball just doesn't have the fame of the NBA. To get more people to attend games, demand has to rise. According to sports writer Joe Denton, people attend live sporting events for five reasons- socializing and networking, halftime shows, promotions and giveaways, team spirit, and impressing peers.[83]

By focusing on these five strategies; the WNBA could increase their fan base, increase ticket sales, increase profit, increase pay for its players, etc. All of that takes time though. While there are several wealthy women athletes, most of them are athletes in individual sports (like tennis or surfing) where sponsorship of individual athletes and athlete-owned marketing (like apparel or

---

[82] The Women's Game. 2019.
[83] Denton. 2016.

house ware) helps increase the individual athletes' incomes. In a team environment, each team has to incorporate a variable of fame when introducing new players.

I learned firsthand during my research study on the role of social media in women's surfing how important social media has become in establishing both fans and wealth in women's sports (which you can read all about in Behind the Break!). In short, women athletes are uniquely dependent on social media as a means of attracting sponsors and building a fan base.

Unfortunately a sports team cannot compete with the charisma of individual athletes that draw far greater social media followings. While the WNBA must certainly continue to acquire talented athletes for winning games, they must also acquire social media moguls capable of delivering fans to games. Fame- more than anything else- will be the necessary variable in growing the WNBA because no matter how successful a team is on the court, they cannot make profits without filling their stadiums.

This is where postmodernism and the importance of the individual become essential. While teamwork is what is certainly needed to deliver a team into the postseason of the WNBA- done so through the modernism of a shared, common goal- a team of women athletes without names that attract fans to attend live games cannot guarantee any team's future. Performance in the Modern sense can secure short-term goals, but performance in the Postmodern is necessary for completing long-term goals. The WNBA cannot survive without its most famous players- end of story.

Chapter 6: Postseason

"Easy to Love" The Jezabels

In the first round of the postseason, the Storm met the Minnesota Lynx in Seattle for their chance to enter the quarterfinals on 11 September. Seattle led the first quarter twenty-nine to twenty-one and maintained their lead into halftime with forty-seven points to forty-one. Seattle continued to lead into the third quarter with a score of sixty-four to fifty-nine before defeating the Lynx eighty-four to seventy-four. Jordin Canada led the Storm with twenty-six points (roughly 3/10), and Damiris Dantas led Minnesota with twenty points (roughly 1/4). Elsewhere in the postseason, Chicago defeated Phoenix.

The Storm left for Los Angeles to play the Sparks on 15 September for the chance to reach the "final four" semifinals. Seattle got an early, marginal lead in the first quarter with twenty-three points to twenty-two; but Los Angeles took the lead going into the half with a score of forty-three to thirty-six. Los Angeles continued to lead in the third quarter with sixty-seven points to Seattle's fifty-eight before defeating Seattle in a final score of ninety-two to sixty-nine. Natasha Howard led the Storm with twenty points (roughly 3/10), and Chelsea Gray led the Sparks with twenty-one points (roughly 1/4).

That was the end of the 2019 season for the Seattle Storm. The team returned to Seattle following their defeat and quietly watched the remainder of the postseason from home as they prepared for competing in foreign leagues. Las Vegas defeated Chicago to enter the semifinals where Washington defeated them to enter the finals. In the Connecticut-Los Angeles semifinal match, Los Angeles seemed to defeat themselves in a game that sent Connecticut to the finals.

During the semifinal series against Connecticut, the Los Angeles General Manager Penny Toler verbally abused her athletes during a halftime break in an attempt to "inspire" them to victory. Instead, morale dropped and the Sparks lost the game. Details emerged after the championship games that revealed the general manager's disastrous halftime speech so infuriated her players that the athletes may have mutinied during the second half of the game as their performance plummeted. The Sparks' coach chose not to play his top players who underperformed in the previous game, and that decision led to a Connecticut win.

Eventually, the Washington Mystics defeated the Connecticut Sun to earn the 2019 championship title. For several parties involved, the season was not the WNBA's best. Several injuries among top players prevented many of the league's most famous players from playing their best- or at all. While "sophomore" athletes were able to get more playing time and earn accolades for their success under extreme conditions- such as the Storm's Jordin Canada and Mercedes Russell- not everyone did well under the pressure.[84]

Fortunately, the Seattle Storm managed to salvage their season with incredible reserve players and coaching staff who were able to regroup and reorganize under their extreme conditions to perform incredibly well for a team few expected to enter the postseason. Without Sue Bird and Breanna Stewart for an entire season, players Natasha Howard, Jordin Canada, and Jewell Loyd formed a powerful trio of points leaders while Crystal Langhorne and Alysha Clarke helped maintain leadership on the court. Dan Hughes fought the odds that a battle of cancer sent against him to return from treatment to lead the team's coaching staff and send the Storm into the postseason.

Unfortunately, Seattle's average attendance per home game dropped in the 2019 season. This was likely from a combination of playing in two separate arenas in home games- with one far outside of Seattle itself- and having the two most famous players out for the entire season. Average attendance dropped to an average of about 7600 per game to drop below 2017's average of 7700.

The largest attendance for a single game- 9000- dropped to a record low highest turnout. The second lowest high was in its second year in 2001 where the lowest high was about 9200 ticket buyers. Alternatively though, their lowest attendance game had roughly 5700 ticket-buyers- the highest lowest attendance since 2012 when the least attended game had 5800 in attendance.

"December" Olivia

---

[84] Martin. 2019.

Following the 2019 season, Alysha Clarke left the US to play for ASVEL Basket in the EuroLeague's 2019/20 season. Natasha Howard left to play for Dynamo Kursk in the EuroLeague, and Jewell Loyd left for Perfumerias Avenida Baloncesto in Spain's women's basketball league. Mercedes Russell left for Australia to play for the Southside Flyers, and Breanna Stewart- at least in name- returned with Natasha Howard to play for Dynamo Kursk in the EuroLeague. Sami Whitcomb left the US to play for Basket Lattes in France's women's league, and Shavonte Zellous returned to Besiktas JK in Turkey's basketball league.

As the WNBA enters its offseason, its leadership needs to consider a major shift in its approach to the future. While the Modernism of sharing a collective goal with the conformity of all of its parts moving like cogs in its proverbial machine, perhaps it is now time for the WNBA to ditch its Modern philosophy for a Postmodern future. Like with several cultures throughout the last five hundred years, modernism has helped solidify the existence and unity of the women's basketball league; but now that pressure to maintain itself is causing its own destruction.

The future of the WNBA's success rests in the power of its individual players. To increase ticket sales, individual athletes need to gain far greater notoriety and fame. To do that, the league must stop treating its players like faceless characters and instead treat them as celebrities in the same way the NBA treats its players. While the collective learning of the modernist WNBA paved the way for knowledge on how to establish foundational success for the contemporary teams in the league, individual teams need to begin establishing unique ways to drive up local support.

At the heart of the philosophy, modernist thought tackles a series of goals by working on one at a time with all parties involved working together on a single, shared goal- or one goal at a time. Postmodernism recognizes the diversity of goals of involved parties as not necessarily all affecting each involved party, and approaches tackling goals as individual parties each independently attempting to solve each party's own goals.

Seattle's attendance at games dropped in 2019 not because of league patterns, but because of the loss of two of their most famous players and moving to two different temporary home stadiums. Minnesota's team should not need to be responsible for helping

Seattle grow their home game audience. To do that, Seattle has to compete with rising attendance for other sports teams in their city- including Reign FC.

Even though the Reign moved from Seattle to nearby Tacoma for the 2019 season- and beyond- the women's soccer team enjoyed a fan base boom following the 2019 women's world cup where fans of women's soccer increased dramatically, and the NWSL found a massive increase in viewership. Women's basketball does not have any major tournament like the FIFA Women's World Cup to create hype for women's basketball at the league level. Although women's basketball exists at the Olympics, the Summer Olympics have never had the power to increase viewership for basketball the way a world cup increases viewership for women's soccer.

Additionally, as the tech industry in Seattle continues to drive out alternative culture- a phenomenon I have watched firsthand while living in the city for eight months during my study- the city's entertainment industry becomes white washed. First I should explain what I mean by this. A friend of mine once explained what he means when he calls people "white."

"Joseph," Tacoma told me, "there are plenty of pasty Irish people I would never call 'white'- and you're one of them. You grew up listening to your family's folk music, you grew up having family reunions on St. Patrick's Day, and you can name like half of the counties in Ireland. But there are Americans with Polish ancestry for example that don't eat the foods their grandparents made when they immigrated here, they don't speak any Polish, and they can't even point to Poland on a map.

"*Those* are white people- and you don't have to be European to be white. I know third generation South Koreans that don't even speak Korean. They eat fast food and drink Starbucks coffee almost everyday, and they listen to whatever music American society tells them to listen to. I know South Koreans that are whiter than you are!"

Essentially, being "white" describes a lack of practiced heritage or unique culture- and Seattle is full of white people. Office buildings for the tech industry in the city replace concert venues, Starbucks replaces local coffee shops, and wealthy coders in slacks and lanyards replace goths with chain nose rings. A city once famous for Nordic immigrants and grunge rock is rapidly becoming a city of bicyclists and tech geeks. As a result, women's sports have taken a beating. While the tech industry imports male software engineers from across the country and abroad, that dramatic increase in male populace increases attendance to men's sporting events while women's sporting event attendance stagnates.

These are not problems the WNBA can- or should attempt to- solve. The Seattle Storm has to find a way to increase attendance in a city that drove them out of their own stadium to make room for a new men's hockey team that doesn't even have a name yet. I remember walking into a cool toy store in downtown Seattle in April during my time in the city while waiting for a Couchsurfer to hang out with. I found a family in Sounders gear and asked them if they also watched women's soccer.

"Oh of course!" the mom replied.

"That's great!" I replied. "So do you go to Reign games?"

"Reign games?" the mom asked.

"Yeah, Seattle's *women's* soccer team?" I followed-up.

"Oh, I didn't know Seattle had a women's team," the mom replied.

I was stunned. (How can a Seattle soccer fan who watches women's soccer not know that her city not only had a team, but had two members of the 2019 USWNT on their roster?) I was so dumbfounded that I literally could not verbally respond. The family just walked away from my very likely floored-chin mouth. As Seattle continues to gain men's sports teams, women's sports in the city will continue to suffer. As league-wide issues- like low pay, referee quality, and travel horrors- continue, the future of the entire WNBA will continue to fall deeper towards collapse.

Throughout the entirety of my study, I kept wanting to find the hope in all of the chaos, but I honestly couldn't. I would love to see women's basketball succeed as a professional sports league in the United States, but maybe it never will. Perhaps the United States just does not value women's basketball. While the Australian and European leagues continue to build on their success, the WNBA is falling apart- and it's not just the WNBA.

Even the USWNT- a women's team in a sport that far exceeds its male equivalent in viewership and revenue- cannot convince US Soccer to provide equal pay to its men's and women's teams. As stories trickle in of countries across the world beginning to pay men and women athletes the same- as with New Zealand and Norway's national soccer teams- perhaps it's time to admit that the future of women's sports is not in the United States. If basketball players can vouchsafe their physical health and earn far better pay in leagues that respect them both as athletes and as women more than they could ever dream of in the US, then perhaps they should leave.

I faced this same struggle during my time in Hawaii. In what I thought would be paradise, what I found was abuse. My manager continuously overworked me without compensation or benefits, a voodoo witch doctor put a curse on me, and I was struggling to find the will to continue when no one seemed to care about me- a blindingly pale dude on an island full of sexy surfer guys. No one valued me in Hawaii. The courageous choice would not have been to stay and try to make it work. The courageous thing to do was what I did- admit I needed help, and go somewhere that might actually care about me.

My job at the hostel in Seattle was challenging, but I never felt like I didn't belong. After only one month, I started to feel like my crazy, nerdy, sexy fencer dude self finally found somewhere where I fit in. Even with all the tech geeks moving into the city, I managed to shake off the voodoo curse and felt warmth again. If the athletes in the WNBA quit en masse and leave in a mass exodus for leagues elsewhere, I will understand completely why they do it.

In the early 2000's, Comedy Central aired a sketch comedy show from comedian Dave Chappelle that included a sketch about tackling issues facing the contemporary world. In the sketch, Chapel's character famously spoke, "Modern problems require modern solutions." The issues facing the WNBA have moved beyond modern into becoming *post*modern problems- and postmodern problems require postmodern solutions.

There are several issues facing the future of the WNBA- from low quality refereeing to low athlete pay. The league not only has to compete with other sports in the United States- including ever expanding men's sports- but increasing viewership of *women's* sports across the world. In short, the United States is on track to no longer be the greatest country in the world for women's sports, and that will be the most difficult postmodern obstacle the league will have to attempt to overcome.

Basketball Playlist

"Cranes in the Sky." Solange. *A Seat at the Table*; Columbia Records. 2016.
"Never Be the Same - Radio Edit." Camila Cabello. *Camila*; Epic Records. 2018.
"Most Girls." Hailee Steinfeld. *Most Girls*; Republic Records. 2017.
"Dancing In The Dark - From The 'Home' Soundtrack." Rihanna. *Home (Original Motion Picture Soundtrack)*; Westbury Road Entertainment, LLC. 2015.
"Love Me Harder." Ariana Grande, The Weeknd. *My Everything (Deluxe)*; Republic Records. 2014.
"Elastic Heart." Sia. *1000 Forms Of Fear (Deluxe Version)*; Monkey Puzzle Records. 2015.
"Fearless." Jasmine Murray. *Jasmine Murray*; Fair Trade Services. 2017.
"Focus." H.E.R. *H.E.R.*; RCA Records. 2017.
"Hands to Myself." Selena Gomez. *Revival (Deluxe)*; Interscope Records. 2015.
"Warrior (Battle Cry Remix)." Hannah Kerr. *Warrior (Battle Cry Remix)*; Black River Christian. 2017.
"Sit Still, Look Pretty (feat. R!OT)." Daya, R!OT. *Sit Still, Look Pretty (feat R!OT)*; ARTBEATZ. 2016.
"Issues." Julia Michaels. *Nervous System*; Republic Records. 2017.
"Starships." Nicki Minaj. *Pink Friday: Roman Reloaded The Re-Up*; Cash Money Records Inc. 2012.
"Roar." Katy Perry. *PRISM (Deluxe)*; Capital Records, LLC. 2013.
"Tightrope (feat. Big Boi) - Big Boi." "Janelle Monae, Big Boi. *The ArchAndroid*; Bad Boy Records, LLC. 2010.
"End Game." Taylor Swift, Ed Sheera, Future. *Reputation*; Big Machine Label Group, LLC. 2017.
"Hold My Hand." Jess Glynne. *Hold My Hand*; Warner Music UK Limited. 2015.
"Hollow." Tori Kelly, Big Sean. *Hollow*; Capitol Records & Schoolboy Records. 2015.
"Gonna Love Me." Teyana Taylor. *K.T.S.E.*; Def Jam Records. 2018.
"Easy To Love." The Jezabels. *She's So Hard*; The Jezabels. 2009.
"December." Olivia. *December*; The TDC Group, Inc. 2016.

Works Cited

"About Alysha Clark." WNBA. 2019. Web.
"About Blake Dietrick." WNBA. 2019. Web.
"About Breanna Stewart." WNBA. 2019. Web.
"About Courtney Paris." WNBA. 2019. Web.
"About Crystal Langhorne." WNBA. 2019. Web.
"About Jewell Loyd." WNBA. 2019. Web.
"About Jordin Canada." WNBA. 2019. Web.
"About Kaleena Masqueda-Lewis." WNBA. 2019. Web.
"About Mercedes Russell." WNBA. 2019. Web.
"About Natasha Howard." WNBA. 2019. Web.
"About Sami Whitcomb." WNBA. 2019. Web.
"About Shavonte Zellous." WNBA. 2019. Web.
"About Sue Bird." WNBA. 2019. Web.
Barcella, Laura. "A Third of Women Student-Athletes Have Mental Health Problems." Vice. 7 August 2017. Web.
"Benefits- Why Sports Participation for Girls and Women." Women's Sports Foundation. 30 August 2016. Web.
Borzi, Pat. "Lynx disappointed with fourth-quarter performance--and poor officiating." *ESPNW*; ESPN. 20 October 2016. Web.
"Breanna Stewart Suffers Ruptured Achilles Tendon." WNBA. 17 April 2019. Web.
Bruggen, Peter and Persaud, Raj. "Are Referees Unfair to Female Players?" Psychology Today. 12 September 2018. Web.
Caron, Emily. "Aces' Liz Cambage Pens Powerful Piece on Mental Health and WNBA Policies." Sports Illustrated. 11 August 2019. Web.
"Cost of living in Lyon, France." Expatistan. 2019.
"Cost of living in Yekaterinburg, Russia." Expatistan. 2019.
Cumming, Sean P.; Malina, Robert M.; and Rogol, Alan D. "Biobanding: A New Paradigm for Youth Sports and Training." *Pediatrics*; AAP New & Journals Gateway. November 2018. Web.
Denton, Joe. "Update: 5 Reasons People Go to Sporting Events." *SCA Promotions*; Event Brite. 31 October 2016. Web.
Durham, Meghan. "Record-setting 2019 tournament concludes with thrilling Women's Final Four in Tampa." NCAA. 23 April 2019. Web.

Engerman, David C.; Gilman, Nils; Haefele, Mark H.; and Latham, Michael E. "Staging Growth: Modernization, Development, and the Global Cold War." University of Massachusetts Press. March 2003. Print.

Evans, Jayda. "Game On! How Women's Basketball Took Seattle by Storm." Sasquatch Books. 2006. Print.

Garrick, Victoria. "Athletes and Mental Health: The Hidden Opponent." *Tedx Talks*; YouTube. 2 June 2017. Video.

Garrick, Victoria. "USC Volleyball Star Talks Eating Disorders and Mental Health in Female Athletes." *Popsugar;* YouTube. 27 March 2018. Video.

Gianbalvo, Emily. "The Seahawks, Mariners, Sounders, Storm and Reign have come together to promote inclusiveness and equality, and organizers on Tuesday said this is the first time a city's professional teams have joined together for this cause." Seattle Times. 20 June 2017. Web.

"Headspace, NBA and WNBA Launch Co-branded Performance Mindset Category Within Meditation and Mindfulness App." WNBA. 12 June 2019. Web.

Helmers, Caden. "Canberra Capitals set their sights on going even bigger." The Sydney Morning Herald. 22 February 2019. Web.

Heshmat, Shahram. "Basics of Identity: What do we mean by identity and why does identity matter?" Psychology Today. 8 December 2014. Web.

"Highlights of the Games." *Modern Olympics*. Olympics.org; International Olympic Committee. 2019. Web.

Jope, Christian. "NBA vs WNBA: Revenue, Salaries, Viewership, Attendance and Ratings." World Sports Network. 18 July 2019. Web.

Kenney, Madeline. "Sky forward Astou Ndour's ejection draws criticism on social media." Chicago Sun Times. 8 September 2019. Web.

Kirpalani, Bela. "The Case for More Female Referees." Washington Square News. 23 April 2018. Web.

Lamonier, Paulana. "The Business of Being A WNBA Player." *Forbes Women*; Forbes. 2 July 2018. Web.

"Las Vegas, NV Rental Market Trends." Rent Café. 2019. Web.

Lemmons, Malcolm. "What Every Athlete Should Know About Athletic Identity." Athlete Network. 2019. Web.

"Major League Baseball supports LGBTQ youth in a big way and the New York Yankees welcome GLAAD Campus Ambassadors to Aaron Judge's Chambers for Spirit Day." GLAAD. 18 October 2019. Web.

Markgraf, Kate. "Why Bad Refs Are A Huge Problem For Women's Soccer." *ESPNW*; ESPN. 18 June 2015. Web.

Martin, Brian. "What You Missed So Far This WNBA Season." WNBA. 15 June 2019. Web.

Martin, Brian. "2019 Season Preview: Seattle Storm." WNBA. 24 May 2019. Web.

Martin, Brian. "2019 WNBA Power Rankings: Week 1." WNBA. 28 May 2019. Web.

Martin, Brian. "2019 WNBA Power Rankings: Week 2." WNBA. 4 June 2019. Web.

Martin, Brian. "2019 WNBA Power Rankings: Week 3." WNBA. 11 June 2019. Web.

Martin, Brian. "2019 WNBA Power Rankings: Week 4." WNBA. 18 June 2019. Web.

Martin, Brian. "2019 WNBA Power Rankings: Week 5." WNBA. 25 June 2019. Web.

Martin, Brian. "2019 WNBA Power Rankings: Week 6." WNBA. 2 July 2019. Web.

Martin, Brian. "2019 WNBA Power Rankings: Week 7." WNBA. 9 July 2019. Web.

Martin, Brian. "2019 WNBA Power Rankings: Week 8." WNBA. 16 July 2019. Web.

Martin, Brian. "2019 WNBA Power Rankings: Week 9." WNBA. 22 July 2019. Web.

Martin, Brian. "2019 WNBA Power Rankings: Week 10." WNBA. 30 July 2019. Web.

Martin, Brian. "2019 WNBA Power Rankings: Week 11." WNBA. 7 August 2019. Web.

Martin, Brian. "2019 WNBA Power Rankings: Week 12." WNBA. 13 August 2019. Web.

Martin, Brian. "2019 WNBA Power Rankings: Week 13." WNBA. 20 August 2019. Web.

Martin, Brian. "2019 WNBA Power Rankings: Week 14." WNBA. 27 August 2019. Web.

Martin, Brian. "2019 WNBA Power Rankings: Week 15." WNBA. 3 September 2019. Web.

Martin, Brian. "Super Sophomores Ready for the Spotlight." WNBA. 14 September 2019. Web.

Martin, Brian. "The Numbers Game: 2019 All-Star Starters." WNBA. 15 July. 2019. Web.

McCauley, Janie. "Storm Stars Own Gay Outreach." *Associated Press*; LA Times. 22 July 2001. Web.

"Mercury's Griner among 5 suspended for fight." ESPN. 13 August 2019. Web.

Murray, Ross. "WNBA Launches LGBT web site, deepens relationship with LGBT fans." GLAAD Media Institute. 21 May 2014. Web.

Oliver, John. "Bias in Medicine: Last Week Tonight with John Oliver (HBO)." *Last Week Tonight*; YouTube. 18 August 2019. Video.

"Out for Sport: The Facts." Equality Network. 2019. Web.

"Partners." WNBA. 2019. Web.

"Perception Is Reality: The Looking-Glass Self." Lesley University. 2019. Web.

"Ratings: WNBA Finals, NBA preseason, NHL." Sports Media Watch. 11 October 2019. Web.

Robinson, LaChina. "WAC with Coach Dan Hughes." *Around the Rim*; ESPN. 20 March 2019. Podcast.

Robinson, LaChina. "Postseason Preview." *Around the Rim*; ESPN. 10 September 2019. Podcast.

"Roman Legions." Know the Romans. Web.

"Seattle, WA Rental Market Trends." Rent Café. 2019.

Sokolove, Michael. "Warrior Girl: Protecting Our Daughters Against the Injury Epidemic in Women's Sports." Simon and Schuster. 2008. Print.

"Stonewall Riots." *History.com*; A&E Television Networks. 2019. Web.

Smith, Michelle. "Inside the W: Offseason Preview." WNBA. 15 January 2019. Web.

"Storm Re-Signs Crystal Langhorne and Mercedes Russell." WNBA. 1 February 2019. Web.

"Ticket Sales Are Vital To AFLW Equity." The Women's Game. 29 October 2019. Web.

Uluc, Olgun. "WNBL and Australian Basketballers' Association secure increased minimum player payment." *Fox Sports Australia*; Fox Sports. 26 March 2019. Web.

Voepel, Mechelle. "Storm's Loyd (ankle) to miss at least 2 weeks." *ESPNW*; ESPN. 28 June 2019. Web.

Voepel, Mechelle. "Why substantially increasing WNBA player salaries is more complex than you think." *ESPNW*; ESPN. 3 July 2018. Web.

Walker, Mollie. "Penn volleyball's season of revolt canceled over 'vulgar' posters." New York Post. 14 November 2019.

Wertheim, Jon. "How Do NBA Franchises Spend Their Revenue? Team Executives Reveal Financial Info." Sports Illustrated. 21 September 2018. Web.

"WNBA's Diana Taurasi and Sue Bird on complicated experience playing in Russia." *30 for 30*; ESPN. 12 November 2019. Podcast.

www.ingramcontent.com/pod-product-compliance
Lightning Source LLC
Chambersburg PA
CBHW051232250726
48655CB00006B/2728